Bring On the Birds

Written and Illustrated by
Susan Stockdale

Special thanks to Dr. Carla Dove of the Smithsonian's National Museum of Natural History for her cheerful support and research assistance. Thanks also to Dr. John Rappole of the Smithsonian's National Zoo and Anne Hobbs of the Cornell Lab of Ornithology for their helpfulness.

Ω

Published by
PEACHTREE PUBLISHERS
1700 Chattahoochee Avenue
Atlanta, Georgia 30318-2112
www.peachtree-online.com

Text and illustrations © 2011 by Susan Stockdale

Art direction by Loraine M. Joyner
Typesetting by Melanie McMahon Ives

The illustrations were created in acrylic on paper.

Bird featured on the cover: Keel-billed Toucan (Southern Mexico, Central America, Colombia, and Venezuela)

Bird featured on the front and back endpapers: Broad-tailed Hummingbird (Western United States, Mexico, and Central America)

Printed in December 2010 by Imago in Singapore
10 9 8 7 6 5 4 3 2 1
First Edition

Library of Congress Cataloging-in-Publication Data

Stockdale, Susan.
    Bring on the birds / written and illustrated by Susan Stockdale. -- 1st ed.
        p. cm.
    ISBN 978-1-56145-560-7 / 1-56145-560-1
    1. Birds--Juvenile literature. I. Title.
    QL676.2.S7535 2011
    598--dc22
                                            2010026893

Swooping birds,

whooping birds,

birds with puffy chests.

Dancing birds,

diving birds,

birds with fluffy crests.

Hanging birds,

hiding birds,

birds with jagged bills.

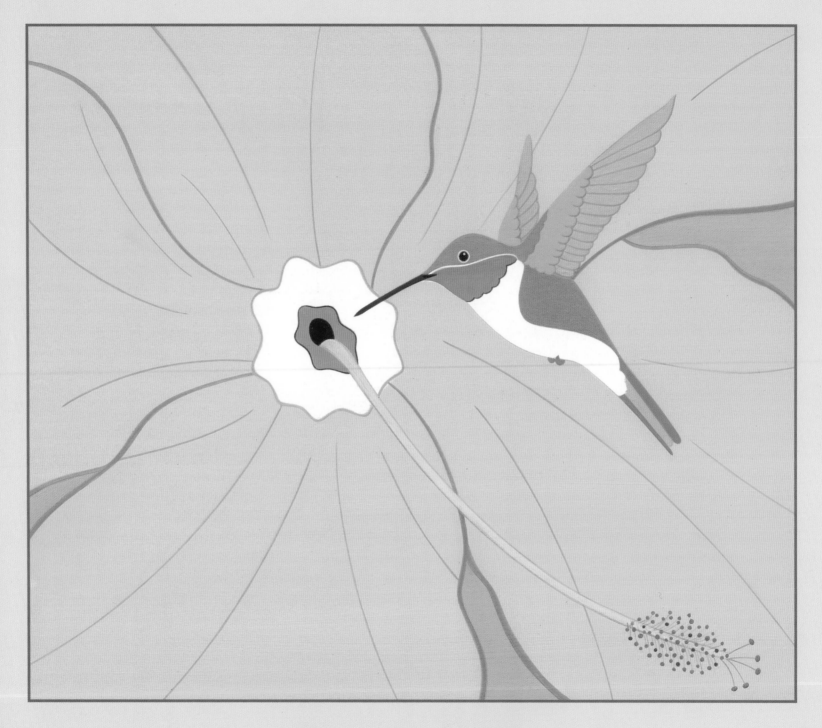

Hummingbirds,

drumming birds,

Skimming birds,

swimming birds,

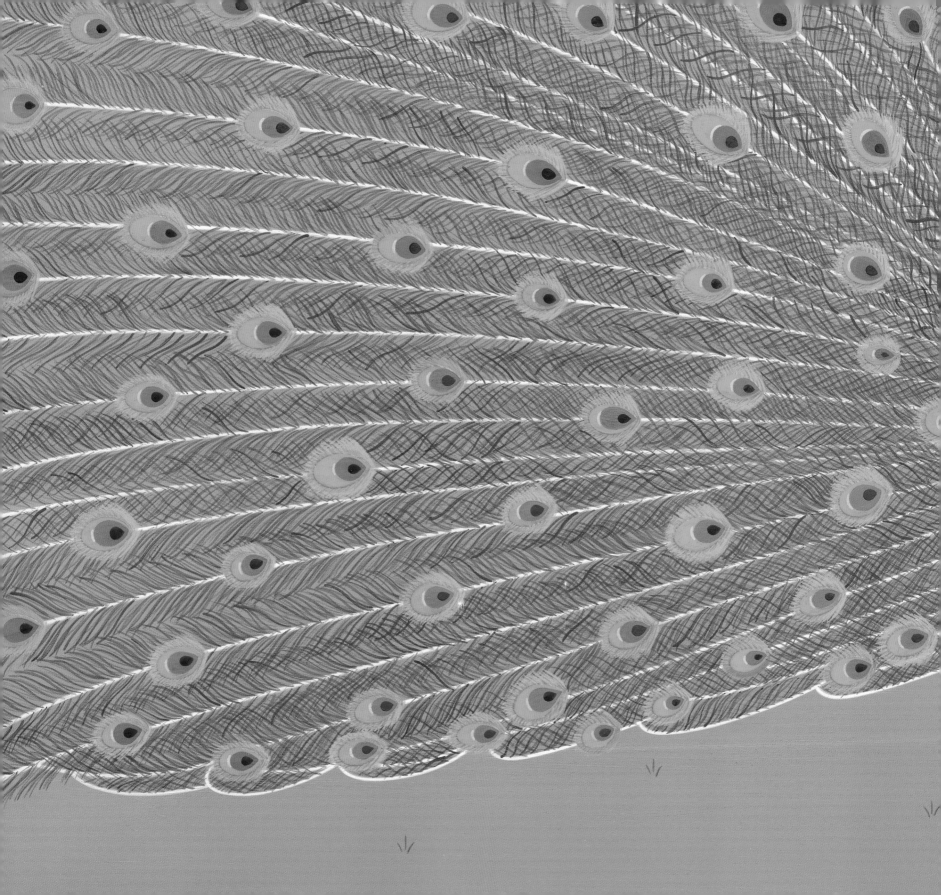

birds with tails held high.

Racing birds,

riding birds,

birds that never fly.

Dull or dazzling colors,

long or little legs.

All of them have feathers,
and all are hatched from eggs.

A nocturnal bird of prey, the **Great Horned Owl** silently swoops down to grab mice and other small animals with its powerful talons. (North, Central, and South America)

The male **Victoria Crowned Pigeon** raises the large crest of feathers on its head and bows to impress a female. (Indonesia and Papua New Guinea)

The **Whooping Crane,** the tallest bird in North America, makes a loud trumpeting call that sounds like a "whoop" during its elaborate mating dance. (North America)

To attract a mate, the male **Blue Bird-of-Paradise** hangs upside down from a branch and spreads his plumes into a shimmering fan. (Papua New Guinea)

The male **Great Frigatebird** has a red-colored throat pouch. When courting, he inflates it like a big balloon. (Pacific, Indian, and Western Atlantic Oceans)

The **White-tailed Ptarmigan** (pronounced *tar*-mih-gan) has coloring that changes with the season. This helps it stay camouflaged and protected from predators. (North America)

The male **Blue-footed Booby** lifts his bright blue feet up and down in a show of footwork to attract a female partner. She joins the dance, following the same movements. (Galapagos Islands)

The **Keel-billed Toucan** has a long bill with jagged edges. It works like a knife to slice chunks of fruit. (Southern Mexico, Central America, Colombia, and Venezuela)

The **Atlantic Puffin** is a powerful diver. Propelled by its strong wings and using its feet as rudders, it can reach depths of 200 feet below the surface of the water to hunt for fish. (North Atlantic Ocean)

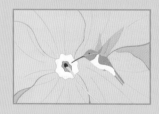

With its long, thin bill, the **Broad-tailed Hummingbird** can reach deep inside flowers to lick up nectar with its tongue. Hummingbirds beat their wings up to 38 times per second! (Western United States, Mexico, and Central America)

The male **Ruffed Grouse** stands on a log and makes a drumming sound by rotating his wings forwards and backwards. The loud sound carries through the forest to help attract a mate. (North America)

Perched on large, grazing mammals, the **Red-billed Oxpecker** eats ticks, flies, and other insects that it finds on their skin. The birds hiss when startled, alerting their hosts to possible danger. (Africa)

The **Red-bellied Woodpecker** uses its sturdy beak to drill holes into trees and branches in search of insects. (North America)

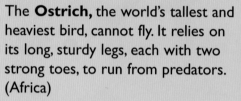

The **Ostrich,** the world's tallest and heaviest bird, cannot fly. It relies on its long, sturdy legs, each with two strong toes, to run from predators. (Africa)

The **Black Skimmer** flies over shallow water with its lower bill immersed, ready to snap up small fish and other prey. (North and South America, Caribbean, and Pacific Coasts)

The male **Indigo Bunting** has brightly colored feathers to attract a female. In contrast, the female bird is drab and plainly colored so she does not stand out while she is on her nest protecting her chicks. (North America)

The **Adelie Penguin** uses its flippers as paddles and steers with its legs to swim through the sea, leaping up out of the water every few seconds to breathe. (Antarctica)

The **Great Blue Heron** has long legs so it can wade into deep water to find food. The **Mottled Duck** has short legs, since it floats in shallow water and forages for food on or just beneath the surface. (North America)

The male **Indian Peafowl,** commonly known as a peacock, displays his dazzling feathers to attract a peahen. (India)

The mother **American Robin** builds a nest and lays three to four blue eggs in it. She sits on the eggs for two weeks to keep them safe and warm. Then the eggs hatch and out come the robin nestlings. (North America)

The **Greater Roadrunner** is a poor flyer but runs faster than any other bird native to North America. It has long, powerful legs to chase after lizards, rodents, and snakes. (United States and Mexico)